WORLD IN
FOCUS

FOCUS ON
Russia

ROB BOWDEN AND GALYA RANSOME

WORLD ALMANAC® LIBRARY

Please visit our web site at: www.garethstevens.com
For a free color catalog describing World Almanac® Library's list of high-quality books
and multimedia programs, call 1-800-848-2928 (USA) or 1-800-387-3178 (Canada).

Library of Congress Cataloging-in-Publication Data available upon request from publisher.

ISBN 978-0-8368-6749-7 (lib. bdg.)
ISBN 978-0-8368-6756-5 (softcover)

This North American edition first published in 2008 by
World Almanac® Library
A Weekly Reader Corporation imprint
200 First Stamford Place
Stamford, CT 06912 USA

This U.S. edition copyright © 2008 by World Almanac® Library. Original edition
copyright © 2007 by Wayland. First published in 2007 by Wayland, an imprint
of Hachette Children's Books, 338 Euston Road, London NW1 3BH, U.K.

Commissioning editor: Nicola Edwards
Editor: Patience Coster
Inside design: Chris Halls, www.mindseyedesign.co.uk
Cover design: Wayland
Series concept and project management by EASI-Educational Resourcing
(info@easi-er.co.uk)
Statistical research: Anna Bowden
Maps and graphs: Martin Darlison, Encompass Graphics

World Almanac® Library editor: Alan Wachtel
World Almanac® Library cover design: Scott M. Krall

Picture acknowledgements. The author and publisher would like to thank the following for allowing their pictures to be reproduced
in this publication:
CORBIS 4 (Pascal Le Segretain), 5 (Sergei Chirikov), 6 (Barry Lewis), 8 (Alfredo Dagli Orti), 9 (Bettmann), 10 (Bettmann), 11 (David
Mdzinarishvili), 12 (Gianni Giansanti), 13 (Peter Blakely), 14 (Staffan Widstrand), 15 (Yann Arthus-Bertrand), 16 (Wolfgang Kaehler), 17
(Alexander Demianchuk), 18 (Robert Wallis), 19 (Gideon Mendel), 20 (Paul A. Souders), 21 (Morton Beebe), 22 (Sergei Karpukhin), 23
(Sergei Karpukhin), 24 (Reuters), 25 (Reuters), 26 (Alexander Natruskin), 27 (Shepard Sherbell), 28 Peter Turnley, 29 Maria Golovnina, 30
Sergie Chirikov, 31 Abraham Nowitz, 32 (Alexander Natruskin), 33 (Peter MacDiarmid), 34 (Yuri Kochetkov), 35 (Hulton-Deutsch
Collection), 36 (Li Gang), 37 (Reuters), 38 (Geoff Arrow), 39 (Steve Raymer), 40 (Buddy Mays), 41 (Richard T. Nowitz), 42 (Gideon Mendel),
43 (Gideon Mendel), 44 (Savintsev Fyodor/ITAR-TASS), 45 (Gideon Mendel), 46 (Stephen Hird), 47 (Le Segretain/Corbis Sygma), 48 and
title page (Reuters/Viktor Korotayev), 49 (Michel Setboun), 50 (Richard Klune), 51 (Dean Conger), 52 (Gideon Mendel), 53 (Steve Raymer),
54 (Robert Wallis), 55 (Vladimir Smolyakov), 56 (Gleb Garanich), 57 (Reuters), 58 (Sergei Chirikov), 59 (Dima Korotayev).

The directional arrow portrayed on the map on page 7 provides only an approximation of north.
The data used to produce the graphics and data panels in this title were the latest available at the time of production.

Printed in China

1 2 3 4 5 6 7 8 9 10 09 08 07

CONTENTS

Cover: The Winter Palace in St. Petersburg was once home to the czars of Imperial Russia but is now part of the world-famous Hermitage Museum.

Title page: Russian children light candles during a Christmas ceremony at a church in the village of Zhilino, near Moscow.

CHAPTER 1

Russia – An Overview

Russia is the world's largest country, stretching from Europe in the west, across Asia, and to the Pacific Ocean in the east. It is also one of the world's most powerful countries, possessing a wealth of natural resources and playing an important role in world politics.

A CENTURY OF CHANGE

The twentieth century was a turbulent time for Russia. At the beginning of the century, the country was ruled by the autocratic Czar Nicholas II, the last of the Romanov czars. In 1917, the people revolted against him. The revolution ushered in the rise of communism under the leadership of Vladimir Lenin. In 1922, the Union of Soviet Socialist Republics (USSR or Soviet Union) emerged as the world's first communist state.

Russia was by far the most dominant republic within the USSR, and Moscow became the Soviet capital (prior to the 1917 revolution, Russia's capital had been St. Petersburg). There followed several decades of rapid industrialization and economic growth, but the Soviet era was marred by violence against anyone who spoke out against authority, and millions of people died as a result. When Germany invaded Russia during World War II, the USSR was drawn into the conflict and sided with the Allied forces to defeat the Nazi regime. By the end of the war in 1945, the USSR had seized control of large areas of eastern Europe and instilled communist principles into many governments there. Politically, the world was divided between communism in the East and democracy in the

▶ A tourist boat travels along the Moscow River toward the Great Kremlin Palace and the Kremlin's cathedrals. Once the powerhouse of the USSR, the Kremlin is now the seat of Russia's democratically elected president.

In spite of its troubles, Russia has retained its position, alongside the United States, as a major player in human space flight. This photo shows a Soyuz rocket being prepared for a mission to the International Space Station (ISS) in March 2006.

West. A so-called "Cold War" followed, in which the USSR and the United States—the world's two superpowers—regarded each other with hostility and suspicion and competed for military dominance and international influence.

In the mid-1970s, the economy of the USSR began to falter, and intellectuals within the country began to speak out against Communism. In spite of attempts by the Communist Party to reverse this process and silence its critics, the situation worsened, and by the early 1980s, the USSR was in crisis. The Soviet leader, Mikhail Gorbachev, attempted to introduce radical new reforms after coming to power in 1985, but these changes did too little and came too late. By the end of 1991, the USSR was so fragmented that Russia and the other Soviet states declared themselves as independent republics.

NEW BEGINNINGS

During the last decade of the twentieth century, Russia underwent dramatic reforms in an attempt to move away from its Communist past and align itself with the free-market economies and democratic political systems that are found in many countries of the world. Russia benefited by inheriting the USSR's immense natural resources (including oil, gas, coal, timber, and numerous minerals), its educated and skilled workforce, and its status in global politics. However, Russia also inherited many problems, including a culture of corruption and bribery and an environment ravaged by years of careless industrialization. There are also political problems, such as factions within Russia—especially in the republic of Chechnya—that seek further autonomy or even independence from Moscow.

Today, in the twenty-first century, the signs are more positive. Russia's economy is growing, corruption has been reduced, and political tensions in the regions are slowly being resolved. Poverty in the country remains high, however, and life expectancy is lower than it was under the USSR. Russia's president, Vladimir Putin, has the firm backing of the population and was reelected with more than 70 percent of the vote in the election of March 2004. Putin intends to bring in further sweeping reforms that will turn Russia into a major world economy. He has already shown his commitment to such pledges, building closer political and economic ties with Europe and the United States to the west, and China and Japan to the east. In spite of these positive signs, analysts think it is too early to say whether Russia has completed the most difficult part of its transformation into a democracy.

 Did You Know?

The city of Kaliningrad (formerly Königsberg) on the Baltic coast became part of Russia at the end of World War II. The area was separated from the main part of Russia in the early 1990s when Lithuania and Belarus became independent. Today, it remains a Russian enclave, strategically important for its access to the Baltic Sea.

Physical Geography Data

- Land area: 6,560,379 sq miles/ 16,995,800 sq km
- Water area: 30,648 sq miles/79,400 sq km
- Total area: 6,591,027 sq miles/ 17,075,200 sq km
- World rank (by area): 1
- Land boundaries: 12,438 miles/20,017 km
- Border countries: Azerbaijan, Belarus, China, Estonia, Finland, Georgia, Kazakhstan, North Korea, Latvia, Lithuania, Mongolia, Norway, Poland, Ukraine
- Coastline: 23,397 miles/37,653 km
- Highest point: Mount Elbrus (18,482 ft/ 5,633 m)
- Lowest point: Caspian Sea (-92 ft/-28 m)

Source: CIA World Factbook

 Did You Know?

Russia is so vast that its territory from east to west crosses 11 time zones.

▶ People out walking in Moscow's snow-covered Gorky Park.

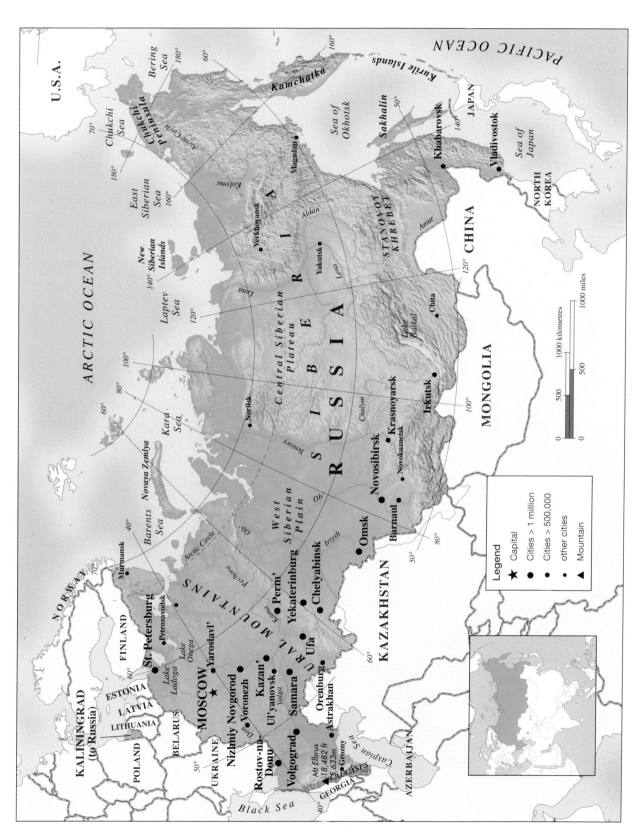

U.S.A.

ARCTIC OCEAN

NORWAY

FINLAND

ESTONIA
LATVIA
LITHUANIA
KALININGRAD
(to Russia)
POLAND
BELARUS
UKRAINE

Bering
Sea

Chukchi
Sea

Chukchi
Peninsula

Arctic Circle

East
Siberian
Sea

New
Siberian
Islands

Laptev
Sea

Kara
Sea

Novaya Zemlya

Barents
Sea

Murmansk

Petrozavodsk

Lake
Onega

Lake
Ladoga

St. Petersburg

Yaroslavl'

MOSCOW

Nizhniy Novgorod

Kazan'

Voronezh

Ul'yanovsk

Samara

Rostov-na-
Donu

Volgograd

Astrakhan

Orenburg

Ufa

Perm'

Yekaterinburg

Chelyabinsk

Omsk

Novosibirsk

Barnaul

Novokuznetsk

Krasnoyarsk

Norilsk

Verkhoyansk

Yakutsk

Chita

Irkutsk

Lake
Baikal

Magadan

Kamchatka

Sakhalin

Khabarovsk

Vladivostok

Kurile Islands

Sea of
Okhotsk

Sea of
Japan

PACIFIC OCEAN

JAPAN

NORTH
KOREA

CHINA

MONGOLIA

KAZAKHSTAN

GEORGIA

AZERBAIJAN

CAUCASUS

Grozny

Mt Elbrus
18,482 ft
5,633m

Caspian Sea

Black Sea

RUSSIA

SIBERIA

Central Siberian
Plateau

West
Siberian
Plain

URAL MOUNTAINS

STANOVOY
KHREBET

Volga
Don
Pechora
Kama
Ob'
Irtysh
Yenisey
Chulym
Lena
Aldan
Amur
Kolyma

Arctic Circle

40°
60°
80°
100°
120°
140°
160°
180°
60°
160°
140°
120°
100°
80°
60°
50°
50°
50°
140°
120°
100°

Legend

★ Capital
● Cities > 1 million
● Cities > 500,000
· other cities
▲ Mountain

1000 kilometres
0   500   1000
1000 miles
0   500

CHAPTER 2

History

Russia has one of the most complex histories of any nation. It has been influenced both by events in Europe and Asia and by the country's own ever-changing boundaries during years of expansion and contraction.

EARLY HISTORY

People have occupied parts of Russia since the second millennium B.C., but little is known about these early settlers. More reliable history dates from the sixth century A.D., when a people called the Slavs occupied parts of eastern and central Europe. Several tribes of eastern Slavs appear to have been the first Slavs to settle in the lands that are now Russia. A possibly legendary account suggests that, in about the ninth century, some of these Slavs were ruled by Prince Rurik, a Viking warrior. The Vikings quickly integrated with the Slavs and formed a state known as Rus (there is some debate about whether this name came from the Vikings or the Slavs) with its capital in Kiev (today the capital of Ukraine). Kiev became an important trading center with trade routes extending north to the Baltic and south to the Black Sea. Besides trade, these routes also had an influence on society and culture. Christianity, for example, came to Russia through trade links with Constantinople (modern-day Istanbul) in around 982 during the reign of Vladimir, grand prince of Kiev.

In the thirteenth century, Russia like much of Asia, came under the control of Mongol Tatars led by Genghis Khan. The Mongol invasion signaled the demise of Kiev and, by the time Mongol rule ended in the early fifteenth century, a new center of power had emerged—Moscow. The void left by the collapse of Mongol Tatar rule resulted in a series of conflicts being fought between Russian princes. Vasily II finally secured the Moscow throne in 1447 and began to consolidate power over other regions of Russia. The relative peace was short-lived, however, and internal wars and political struggles continued until the early seventeenth century, when the Romanov family came to the throne.

FROM EMPIRE TO REVOLUTION

The Romanov czars oversaw a period of Russian empire building, during which the borders of control were expanded into new territories. However, the Russian empire was slow to develop economically and politically,

◀ A portrait of Peter the Great, who was czar of Russia from 1682 to 1725 and one of the main figures in the period of Russian empire building.

Focus on: The Last Czar

In 1917, Czar Nicholas II abdicated and was imprisoned in Tobolsk, in northwest Russia, with his wife, Alexandra, their four daughters, and their son. Not content with his fall from power, the Communist revolutionary Bolsheviks who had seized control of Russia decided that the czar had to die. In July 1918, Nicholas II and his family were executed in the house of a Yekaterinburg merchant. So bitter was the feeling against the royal family that their bodies were doused in acid, burned, and thrown into a mine shaft. In 1970, their remains were discovered, and they were recovered in 1991. DNA tests conducted with living relatives of the Romanov family proved the remains were genuine. In 1998, the family was buried alongside other members of the Romanov family in St. Petersburg. In 2000, Czar Nicholas II and his family were canonized, or officially declared to be saints, by the Russian Orthodox Church.

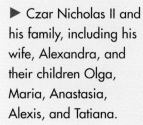

▶ Czar Nicholas II and his family, including his wife, Alexandra, and their children Olga, Maria, Anastasia, Alexis, and Tatiana.

and this led to discontent among its subjects. In 1861, this discontent led Czar Alexander II to abolish existing patterns of land ownership under which most Russian peasants had been living virtually as serfs. This gesture failed to end the discontent, and members of a revolutionary movement began to plan ways in which they might overthrow the royal family. In 1881, after several attempts, revolutionary terrorists assassinated Czar Alexander II but failed to overthrow the monarchy.

The successor to the throne, Czar Alexander III, managed to resist the revolutionaries until his death in 1894, upon which his son, Nicholas II, came to power. Czar Nicholas II was a weak ruler and was heavily influenced by his wife, Alexandra Fyodorovna, and a Siberian monk named Grigory Rasputin. Nicholas II had an opportunity to pacify the revolutionaries by turning Russia into a modern constitutional monarchy with an elected parliament and the czar as head of state. A parliament was established, but it had few real powers.

Nicholas II remained in control of the country and of the Russian army. World War I had a disastrous economic effect on Russia and led to widespread discontent, which expressed itself in a series of workers' strikes that began in 1915 and became progressively bigger and more political. A turning point came in January 1917, when the army was sent to Moscow to disperse workers who were calling for an end to the power and domination of the czar. The army refused to obey orders and joined the workers in calling for change, and its example was soon followed in other parts of Russia. In February 1917, the Duma (Russian parliament) formed a provisional government to try to restore social order, but it was weak and failed to bring stability. In the same month, Czar Nicholas II was forced to abdicate his throne, bringing the 300-year rule of the Romanov dynasty to an end.

THE DAWN OF COMMUNISM

In October 1917, the Bolshevik Party—under its leader, Vladimir Lenin—overthrew the provisional government and seized control of St. Petersburg. However, the Bolsheviks did not have immediate control over the vast lands of Russia, and a bitter civil war erupted in which Lenin and his Red Army gradually crushed

any opposition. The civil war ended in 1921. The Union of Soviet Socialist Republics (USSR), or the Soviet Union—the world's first Communist state—formed the next year. Under communism, almost all aspects of life were brought under the central control of the ruling Communist Party. This model would later be followed by other Communist countries and became the basis of the Cold War between those countries supporting Communism and those supporting democracy.

Lenin's death in 1924 led to yet another power struggle for the leadership of the country. Two of the main contenders for this were Leon Trotsky, who had helped lead the Red Army during the civil war, and the general secretary of the Communist Party, Joseph Stalin. They and others disagreed on key policies about the future of the USSR, but Stalin's influence eventually triumphed and his power became

▼ Vladimir Lenin, the Russian Communist leader, addresses a mass meeting in a Moscow square in about 1920. Lenin asked the Russian people to remain united during what were turbulent times.

absolute by the late 1920s. He is remembered as a ruthless leader who led the country through a period of rapid industrialization. He also supervised the reorganization of Soviet agriculture into state, controlled "collective farms." Those who opposed Stalin risked persecution and death, and it is claimed that as many as 25 million people died during his "reign of terror."

At the outbreak of the World War II in 1939, Stalin agreed a pact of nonaggression with Nazi Germany, which enabled the USSR to take control of Latvia, Lithuania, Estonia, and half of Poland. However, after German forces invaded Russia in 1941, Stalin joined the Allies against the Nazis. Once involved, the Soviet forces were engaged in some of the war's most ferocious battles, and an estimated 25 million Soviet citizens were killed. The Soviet involvement proved vital in the eventual overthrow of the Nazis and had repercussions for the next 50 years.

After World War II ended, Europe begain to rebuild itself. The Soviet Union remained in control of much of eastern Europe, and a political divide emerged between Communist governments of the east and the democratic governments of the west. This political division became known as the "Iron Curtain" and was symbolized by the construction of the Berlin Wall, which divided the German city into a democratic sector (West Berlin) and a Communist sector (East Berlin). As these divisions became more apparent, a new type of war emerged. The Cold War focused not on physical conflict but on military threats and the building of huge stores of nuclear weapons to intimidate the opposing side. Technological superiority was another important aspect of the

▲ Joseph Stalin was a brutal Soviet dictator, but his memory is honored here by a loyal Georgian Communist, who carries the leader's portrait to mark the anniversary of Stalin's death.

 Did You Know?

In 1962, Soviet premier Nikita Khrushchev (leader 1953–1964) brought the world to the brink of nuclear war. He provided the USSR's Communist ally, Cuba, with nuclear weapons to protect itself from possible attack by the United States. This led to a tense standoff between the USSR and United States (under President John F. Kennedy). This conflict ended with the USSR withdrawing nuclear weapons from Cuba in return for a promise from the United States never to invade the Communist country.

Cold War, most evident in the "space race" between the USSR and the United States. In 1957, the USSR succeeded in launching the first satellite, and in 1961, it became the first nation to launch a manned space flight.

THE BEGINNING OF THE END

In spite of the USSR's success in the space race, the Communist system was failing to keep up with the demands of daily life. By the 1970s, shops were often without goods, and lines formed for even basic supplies. At the same time, the Soviet government began to lose its controlling grip on the the media, and people became more aware of life beyond the Iron Curtain. The Communist Party faced growing criticism from intellectuals and some members of the wider population, and it reacted by imprisoning or deporting its critics.

By the early 1980s, the USSR was in crisis because of further decline in its economy, and its leadership was in turmoil. An element of stability returned in 1985, when Mikhail Gorbachev became premier of the USSR. Gorbachev recognized the need for urgent economic and political reforms and introduced two new policies: perestroika, a restructuring of politics and the economy, and glasnost, or openness about political ideas and what was happening in the USSR. In spite of ambitious plans, perestroika was poorly implemented, while glasnost strengthened the arguments of those already disillusioned with Communism and the USSR. As discontent grew, several parts of the Soviet Union sought to break away from Moscow. In 1990, Gorbachev authorized the use of military force to try to keep the union intact. However, this further rallied people behind their individual republics and marked the beginning of the end for the USSR.

THE EMERGENCE OF RUSSIA

Soviet and Russian history changed a great deal in 1991. Boris Yeltsin, the newly elected president of Russia (at that point a republic within the USSR), emerged to challenge Gorbachev. Yeltsin argued for an independent Russia and an end to Communism. In August 1991, he put down an attempted coup by communist hard-liners, an event that greatly weakened Gorbachev's standing. Gorbachev

▶ Soviet leader Mikhail Gorbachev was the architect of glasnost and perestroika, two policies designed to save the troubled USSR. In the end, they brought about its demise.

► Vladimir Putin (center, without a hat) visits the Tomb of the Unknown Soldier in 1999. Putin was elected president in March 2000.

remained in power, but Yeltsin became politically stronger and used his position to undermine Gorbachev's authority by banning the Communist Party in Russia and seizing all of its property. On December 25, 1991, Gorbachev resigned, and on December 31, the USSR officially ceased to exist. Russia emerged from the fallen USSR as an independent republic with Boris Yeltsin as its president. Fourteen other former Soviet republics also became independent nations.

RUSSIA SINCE 1991

Yeltsin inherited a declining economy and a country full of political and social tensions. The 1990s were plagued with problems including mass unemployment, rising poverty, growing crime, and ethnic conflicts. Yeltsin pursued aggressive reform policies. He also launched military action against a breakaway faction in the southern district of Chechnya. Under intense pressure, Yeltsin's health also began to deteriorate, and he suffered a series of major

heart attacks. By the end of the 1990s, Yeltsin had overseen a ceasefire in Chechnya. There were some signs of economic recovery, but Russia still faced an uphill struggle. In late 1999, Yeltsin resigned and appointed his young prime minister, Vladimir Putin, as his successor.

Under Putin, economic and political reforms continued. Some people believed these reforms handed too much control to the president and his appointed deputies, but others applauded Putin for attempting to stamp out corruption within the country's extensive political system. Russia's economy has boomed under Putin's presidency and is bringing record levels of foreign revenue into Russia, thanks to its vast energy reserves. Putin has also raised the profile of Russia in global affairs. He has become a well-respected statesman, with firm opinions. For example, Putin was against the manner in which the United States led the invasion of Iraq, in spite of pledging his full support for the international war on terrorism.

CHAPTER 3

Landscape and Climate

Russia covers a vast area extending from the Baltic Sea in the west to the Pacific Ocean in the east and from the Arctic in the north to the Caspian Sea in the south. Covering 6,591,027 square miles (17,075,200 square kilometers), Russia's area is almost twice that of the United States and nearly 70 times larger than Britain. Russia's immense area includes a wide range of landscapes and several different climates.

TUNDRA AND TAIGA

Much of Russia consists of vast and mainly flat plains. In the far north, this landscape is known as tundra, a Russian term meaning "treeless heights." As its name suggests, the tundra is a treeless habitat with a generally harsh climate and extremely low winter temperatures of less than -22°F (-30°C). Beneath the surface of the tundra, there is generally a layer of permanently frozen subsoil, called permafrost, which can be up to 4,593 feet (1,400 meters) deep. The very harsh conditions mean that the tundra is dominated by lichens, mosses, grasses, and small shrubs. South of the tundra lies the taiga, which is a forest covering most of northern and eastern Russia. The taiga also experiences a harsh climate, with long, cold winters and temperatures below freezing for at least six months of the year. Summers are short,

▼ A herd of reindeer (also known as caribou) grazes on the tundra plains of Siberia on the Chukchi Peninsula.

▲ An aerial view of the taiga landscape near Tjumen. Taiga (also known as boreal forest) covers much of northern and eastern Russia.

warm, and wet. During this season, the forests thrive with insect and bird life. Besides coniferous tree species such as pine, spruce, larch, and hemlock, taiga vegetation is made up of mainly mosses, lichens, and grasses.

DIVIDING MOUNTAINS

Russia is split geographically by the Ural Mountains, or Urals, that extend north to south for about 1,550 miles (2,500 kilometers) and are traditionally considered the dividing point between Europe, to the west, and Asia, to the east. The land to the east of the Urals as far as the Pacific Ocean is known as Siberia and makes up about two-thirds of Russia. Dominated by tundra and taiga, Siberia has a much smaller population than other parts of

Russia and is less developed. Siberia is important to the Russian economy, however, because it is the location of the majority of Russia's mineral wealth, especially in its northern regions. The Urals themselves are also rich in mineral resources and support a thriving industrial economy.

 Did You Know?

The taiga biome, or habitat, covers a greater area than any other land-based habitat. From Russia, the taiga extends into Scandinavia. Taiga is also present in North America, where it is more commonly known as boreal forest.

Russia's other great dividing mountains are the Caucasus Mountains, which run along Russia's southern border with Georgia and Azerbaijan. The mountains extend for about 750 miles (1,200 km) between the Black Sea, in the west, and the Caspian Sea, in the east. The Russian portion of the Caucasus Mountains includes Mount Elbrus, which at about 18,482 feet (5,633 m) is the highest peak in both Russia and Europe. The name Elbrus refers to the mountain's twin peaks. Elbrus's eastern summit is slightly lower than its western one.

LAKES AND RIVERS

The Volga River in western Russia is the longest in Europe, at about 2,194 miles (3,530 km). The Volga's course flows through the most populated region of Russia, and about half the country's total population lives within its river basin. The Volga and its major tributary, the Kama River, are extensively used by humans, with eleven hydroelectric power (HEP) stations and numerous artificial reservoirs used for water supply and irrigation.

The longest river in Russia is the Lena. It flows northward through western Siberia for 2,734 miles (4,400 km) before discharging into the Arctic Ocean. The Lena's waters are not yet intensively used but have several times the HEP potential of the Volga.

Lake Baikal, in eastern Russia, is the world's deepest freshwater lake. It has a maximum depth of 5,715 feet (1,742 m) and contains one-fifth of all of the world's surface freshwater. It is also the oldest freshwater lake, dating back

Did You Know?

The Volga River system is fed by a network of about 151,000 rivers and streams that have a total length of 357,017 miles (574,536 km). This makes it one of the world's largest river systems.

▼ A train on the Trans-Siberian Railway passes by Lake Baikal, the world's deepest and oldest freshwater lake and a site of great ecological importance.

20 million to 25 million years. Its uniqueness means it has earned classification and protection as a World Heritage site. In spite of this status, the lake suffers pollution from surrounding industries that include a cellulose factory and a paper mill. In 1971, Russia's government introduced policies to protect the lake, but pollution remains an issue.

CLIMATE

Russia's enormous territory means that its climate is incredibly varied. In the broadest terms, the country's northern latitudes are colder than its southern latitudes, but the entire country is prone to extremes of temperature and generally harsh weather conditions during the long, cold winter months. Summers are short and can be very hot in the south, with temperatures reaching up to 104°F (40°C). The majority of Russia's people live in the central regions of European Russia, where conditions are more balanced and extremes of temperature less pronounced.

▲ A driver steers a carriage across Dvortsovaya Square in St. Petersburg during a winter snowstorm.

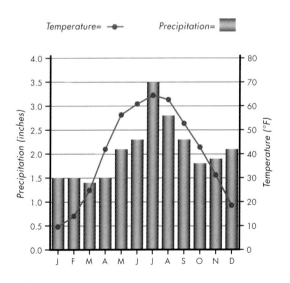

▲ Average monthly climate conditions in Moscow

The Caspian Sea

Russia is one of five countries sharing the waters of the Caspian Sea, the world's largest enclosed body of water. At 149,150 sq miles (386,400 sq km) in area, it is larger than Japan. The sea is famous for its sturgeon fish whose eggs, or caviar, are a renowned delicacy and one of the world's most expensive foods. About 80 percent of the global caviar supply comes from the Caspian Sea. The Caspian Sea also has significant oil and gas reserves beneath the sea bed and surrounding shores. This mineral wealth is the cause of ongoing political disputes over territorial rights between Russia and the other countries (Kazakhstan, Turkmenistan, Iran, and Azerbaijan) that share the sea.

 Did You Know?

The lowest ever temperature in Russia was recorded in Verkhoyansk in 1933. It was about -90°F (-68°C).

CHAPTER 4

Population and Settlements

Russia's population is dispersed across its vast territory and includes a diversity of ethnic groups among whom 100 languages are spoken. In global terms, Russia's 2005 population of 143.2 million people makes it the eighth most populous nation in the world.

POPULATION DECLINE

Up until 1989, the population of the USSR had been steadily growing. In post-1989 Russia, however, the general pattern has been a gradual decline in population, and this is a trend predicted to continue into the future. There are many contributing factors to this trend, such as the high mortality rate among Russian men. Work-related accidents, alcoholism, and poor diet and health care are the main reasons given for this. The average male life expectancy at birth fell from 65 in 1988 to just 58.8 in 2003.

Poor health care in general means that Russia's infant mortality rate (an important measure of health-care quality) is higher in Russia, at 16 deaths per 1,000 live births, than in other developed nations such as Britain or the United States, where it is 5 and 7 deaths per 1,000 live births, respectively. The problem is especially acute in Russia's more remote regions, where infant mortality rates as a result of infectious diseases or pneumonia may be several times higher than those of the more developed western region.

Russia's maternal mortality rate is also high, at about three times that of Britain or the United States, and is often the result of complications that can occur during abortion procedures. In the Soviet Union during the twentieth century, poor contraceptive practices meant that abortion was often the main method of birth control. Even today, abortion rates in Russia remain among the highest in the world and contribute directly to the country's low birth rate.

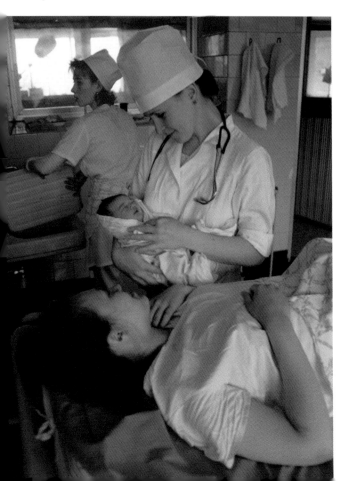

◀ A nurse cradles a newborn baby in a Moscow maternity hospital. Proper facilities such as this hospital are helping to reduce Russia's relatively high maternal and infant mortality rates.

Some population experts predict that Russia's population decline could leave it with fewer than 100 million people by the middle of the twenty-first century. Under these circumstances it would be difficult to maintain a modern

▲ At Bol'shoye Goloustnoye (near Lake Baikal), a boy takes the family cow to drink from a watering hole. Russia's declining population could threaten rural livelihoods; the current generation is aging, and many younger people are moving to the cities.

Population Data

- Population: 143.2 million
- Population 0-14 yrs: 16%
- Population 15-64 yrs: 70%
- Population 65+ yrs: 14%
- Population growth rate: -0.6%
- Population density: 21.7 per sq mile/ 8.4 per sq km
- Urban population: 73%
- Major cities: Moscow 10,654,000
  St. Petersburg 5,312,000

Source: United Nations and World Bank

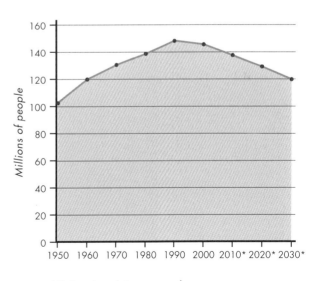

* Projected population

▲ Population growth, 1950–2030

developed economy in such a large country. Other experts believe that improvements in the country's economy and standard of living, together with greater political stability and freedom, will encourage a return to positive population growth within this period. The impact of a declining population is being partially offset by immigrants from former Soviet republics, many of whom are Russians or Russian speakers. The largest numbers of immigrants to Russia are from Armenia, Azerbaijan, Georgia, and Tajikistan.

ETHNIC DIVERSITY

About 80 percent of the country's people are ethnically Russian and speak Russian as their only language. Among the remaining 20 percent are more than 100 ethnic groups, some of whom speak languages that are almost extinct. All but the few groups living in remote areas also speak Russian. Russia's main ethnic minorities are Tatar (3.8 percent), Ukrainian (2 percent), Bashkir (1.2 percent), Chuvash (1.1 percent), Chechen (0.9 percent), and Armenian (0.8 percent).

DISTRIBUTION AND SETTLEMENT

Taken as a whole, Russia has a very low population density of just 21.7 people per sq mile (8.4 per sq km). This is almost four times lower than the United States and over 30 times lower than Britain. Because so much of Russia's environment is hostile to settlement, population distribution is far from even. In fact, about 80 percent of the country's population lives in the roughly 20 percent of its land area in the central and southern parts of European Russia. In the Moscow region, population density is much higher than average, at about 360 per sq mile (140 people per sq km). In contrast, the Taymyr region of Siberia has a population density of just 0.11 per sq mile (0.05 people per sq km).

About 73 percent of Russians live in urban areas. Moscow and St. Petersburg are the major cities, with Moscow alone having nearly 8 percent of the country's population. Besides Moscow and St. Petersburg, 11 cities have populations of between 1 million and 2 million. Of these, only two—Omsk and Novosibirsk—are in Siberia.

▶ A Koryak grandmother and her granddaughter in a reindeer herding village in the Magadan region of northeast Russia. The Koryak are one of Russia's many ethnic minorities.

▲ An aerial view over Moscow, the largest city in Russia and one of the most densely populated regions of the country. Many people in Moscow live in high-rise apartment buildings.

MOVING EAST

Migration has been an important feature of Russia's population distribution for hundreds of years. One of the main migratory patterns has been of people moving eastward into Siberia from the more crowded central regions of European Russia. These European regions have a long history of settlement. People crossed the Ural Mountains into Siberia beginning in the late sixteenth century, as Russia sought to extend its boundaries. During the Soviet period, this movement of people continued as the economic development of Siberia's natural resources became a priority. With the continuing development of Siberian energy and mineral resources, there remains an eastward flow of people into Siberia.

Focus on: Emigration

Russia has experienced several waves of emigration over the last one hundred years as people sought to flee the effects of revolution, war, and the emergence of Communism. In the second half of the twentieth century, a substantial wave of religion-based emigration took place when many Russian Jews emigrated to Israel. About 2 million Jews left Russia (then the USSR) between 1945 and 1991. Since the collapse of the USSR, emigration from the country has been primarily for economic reasons, with many educated and skilled Russians leaving in search of better paying jobs and a higher standard of living. Expatriate Russian communities are today well established in Europe, the United States, and eastern Asia.

CHAPTER 5

Government and Politics

At the start of the twentieth century, Russia was still ruled as an autocratic empire led by a czar who made all key decisions and whose word was law. In 1905, however, dissatisfaction with this system triggered a process of radical political changes, and Nicholas II was forced to concede some of his powers and establish the beginnings of a constitutional monarchy. A government and parliament, the Duma, was formed and granted powers to oversee the introduction of all new laws. In reality, power remained with Nicholas, the last of Russia's czars, who would simply close down the parliament if its members disagreed with him. By February 1917, however, mismanagement of the country had led to the forced abdication of Nicholas II in what became the first phase of the Russian Revolution.

COMMUNISM AND THE SOVIET UNION

In the second phase of the Russian Revolution, an alliance of workers' councils (soviets) seized control of the country from the weak provisional government in October 1917. This marked the start of the Communist era and, by 1922, the Union of Soviet Socialist Republics (USSR, or Soviet Union) had been formed. In the Soviet Union, the Communist Party of the Soviet Union (CPSU) was the only political party and its representatives controlled all aspects of government and decision making. CPSU members occupied positions of authority in all official institutions in the country.

Within the CPSU, the politburo (the principal policy-making committee) was the elite group

▶ Russian activists from extreme left-wing organizations bear red flags as they march through central Moscow in September 2005 to protest the "capitalist" policies of the Russian government and president.

with—in theory, at least—the highest authority to make decisions. Also important were the central committee and the secretariat, which controlled party policy and administration. In spite of these structures, the greatest power lay with the general secretary. This was particularly so from the mid-1920s until 1953, when Joseph Stalin held the position as a virtual dictator. After Stalin's death, efforts were made to allocate power more widely, but the post of general secretary remained of major importance and status until the collapse of the Soviet Union in 1991.

A NEW ERA

Since 1991, Russia has been governed as a federal republic, with a president as the chief of state. Russia's president is elected by popular vote and serves a four-year term. The government itself is headed by a premier who is appointed by the president with the approval of the Duma (the prerevolutionary name still used for the lower chamber of parliament). The premier also acts in place of a vice-president if the president becomes unfit for office or dies.

The Duma is made up of 450 members who are elected every four years by popular vote. An upper chamber of parliament, the Federation Council, has 178 members appointed by the top legislative and executive officials in Russia's 89 federal administrative regions. Each region appoints two members.

Did You Know?

Women are poorly represented in Russian politics. For example, only 44 members of the 450-member Duma are female. In the Federation Council, representation is even lower, with just 9 women among its 178 members.

▲ The deputies of Russia's Duma pose for a photograph following one of their state meetings.

The political division of Russia into 89 federal administrative units has changed little since Soviet times. Each unit is controlled by a governor appointed by the president. The governors have considerable powers but must ensure that local policies conform to those of the president. The cities of Moscow and St. Petersburg are independent of surrounding regions and are governed by elected mayors.

REFORM AND RESISTANCE

Russia's first democratically elected president was Boris Yeltsin, who held power from 1991 until his resignation at the end of 1999. Yeltsin introduced radical political and economic reforms to modernize Russia, but these met with significant resistance from the Congress of the People's Deputies, an assembly of representatives of local councils that had survived from Soviet times. In 1993, there was an attempted coup against Yeltsin in Moscow. However, the security service and army rallied to his cause and, using force, regained control of the parliament buildings. Opposition to Yeltsin was crushed in a ten-day conflict during which, according to the government, 187 people were killed and 437 people were wounded, almost all of them anti-Yeltsin protesters. With his authority reestablished, Yeltsin introduced a new constitution in 1993 and proceeded with far-reaching reforms to restructure and open up Russia's economy. Vladimir Putin, who succeeded Yeltsin as president, has continued with these reforms, but concerns have been expressed during his presidency about the reemergence of state intervention. Nevertheless,

Focus on: Presidential Power

In spite of political reforms, Russia's president retains substantial independent powers. The president can pass decrees without consent from parliament and is the head of both the country's armed forces and its national security council. Russia's president also appoints all the main state officials, who are then able to exercise their powers throughout the country. Officially, the president is not affiliated with any political party, but Vladimir Putin enjoys strong support from the United Russia Party, which dominates the country's contemporary politics. Some political commentators believe that the president has too much power in Russia. Under Putin, there has been an increase in state control of the economy, particularly in those sectors that are powerful, vast, and lucrative, such as the energy industry.

▶ Boris Yeltsin (center, holding a paper) delivers a speech while standing atop an armored vehicle outside a government building in Moscow. He was speaking out against the attempted coup that took place against Gorbachev in August 1991.

► Chechen protesters in Berlin, Germany, stand in front of a poster of Russian president Vladimir Putin to register their opposition toward his policy in Chechnya. The protest in February 2003 was timed to coincide with a two-day state visit to Germany by Putin.

Putin was reelected as president with 71 percent of the vote in March 2004.

THE CHECHNYA PROBLEM

In November 1991, the republic of Chechnya declared itself independent of Russia under the leadership of Dzhokhar Dudayev, a former Soviet general. Russia refused to accept the secession of Chechnya and supported groups opposed to Dudayev in attempting to regain control of Chechnya. These attempts failed, and in December 1994, Russia sent in its military to reclaim Chechnya. More than two years of war followed, until a ceasefire was reached in May 1997. However, the ceasefire was weak and fighting resumed in 1999. The conflict also spread, with Chechen terrorists carrying out bombings and hostage sieges elsewhere in Russia. Hundreds of people were killed in these actions, and Russia launched antiterrorism actions in Chechnya in an

effort to hunt down the killers. As some stability returned, a referendum was held in 2003 that gave Chechnya greater powers but kept it as part of the Russian federation. In 2004, however, the new pro-Russian president of Chechnya, Akhmad Kadyrov, was murdered in a bomb attack. In the same year, a siege by Chechen terrorists at a school in the Russian town of Beslan, on the Chechen border, led to the deaths of 331 people, half of them children. New elections were held in 2005, but violence and opposition to Russia has spread beyond Chechnya into neighboring provinces. Bringing stability to this region is one of Russia's most significant political challenges.

 Did You Know?

At least 100,000 people are believed to have died in the conflict in Chechnya, and up to 500,000 people have been forced to flee their homes.

CHAPTER 6

Energy and Resources

Several decades ago, the Soviet Union and the United States were the world's two great superpowers. Today, Russia has lost much of the political and military might it used to have as the Soviet Union, but it is reemerging in the twenty-first century as a new type of superpower—an energy superpower.

NATURAL GAS

Russia has more proven natural gas reserves than any other country, accounting for 27 percent of the global total in 2005. It is also the world's biggest producer (22 percent of global total) and exporter (30 percent of global exports) of natural gas, with a particularly dominant position in the European markets. For example, Germany, the world's third largest economy, depends on Russia for 41 percent of its natural gas imports, while France and Italy obtain about one-third of their gas imports from Russia. The significance of Russia's gas supplies became clear in January 2006, when a dispute with Ukraine over the price it paid for Russian gas led to the risk of Europe's gas supplies, which are carried via a pipeline through Ukraine, being cut off. The dispute was resolved, and gas flows were only slightly disrupted, but the incident made it very clear that many countries depend on Russian gas. This dependency is likely to increase as other sources run out. Energy experts estimate that, by 2020, the European Union (EU) may depend on Russian gas to meet as much as 45 percent of its total energy needs.

▼ A crane lifts up a segment of the Baltic Sea Gas Pipeline near the town of Babayevo, in the Vologda region, about 404 miles (650 km) northeast of Moscow. The laying of this new pipeline was started by Gazprom in December 2005. The pipeline will take Siberian gas directly to Germany across the floor of the Baltic Sea.

OIL

Russia has about 6 percent of the world's known oil reserves and is the world's second biggest oil producer, after Saudi Arabia. It accounted for 12 percent of global oil production in 2005. Oil production fell in the first years of post-Soviet Russia, but with high world prices for oil, Russia's production has risen again to almost maximum levels. Over 70 percent of Russia's crude oil is exported, and two-thirds of this goes to Europe, where it is used primarily to heat homes. Russia also refines oil and has about 40 oil refineries. Many of these, however, are in need of modernization and repair because they were neglected during the Soviet period.

COAL

Russia's coal reserves make up about 17 percent of the world total. Only the United States has greater coal reserves. Like the oil industry, the

▶ Most of Russia's oil reserves are located in Siberia. This oil derrick stands in the Vazeyskaya Oil Field.

Energy Data

- Energy consumption as % of world total: 6.2%
- Energy consumption by sector (% of total):
  Industry: 33.7
  Transportation: 20.1
  Agriculture: 3.5
  Services: 6.3
  Residential: 33.1
  Other: 3.3
- CO_2 emissions as % of world total: 6.4
- CO_2 emissions per capita in tons per year: 11.2

Source: IEA

Focus on: Gazprom

Russia's gas industry is controlled by a partly (38 percent) state-owned monopoly called Gazprom that was established in 1993 to take over state gas production from the Soviet era. Gazprom produces nearly 90 percent of Russia's gas, owns 60 percent of known reserves, and controls the pipelines for the distribution and export of Russian gas. Economically, Gazprom is responsible for about 8 percent of Russia's GDP and 20 percent of its federal budget. It also employs about 300,000 people in its direct and subsidiary operations.

coal industry was neglected during the last years of the Soviet era. This, combined with falling global demand for coal during the 1990s, led to a slump in production from about 344 million tons (312 million metric tons) in 1992 to 236 million tons (214 million metric tons) by 1998. Russia's coal industry has since been restructured and growing demand for coal in Asia brought production to about 298 million tons (270 million metric tons) in 2004.

ELECTRICITY PRODUCTION

Russia not only produces large quantities of energy, it is also a major energy consumer— the third largest in the world. Electricity production in Russia comes primarily from its vast fossil fuel resources. Russian natural gas alone generates more than 44 percent of its electricity. HEP facilities, such as those on the Volga River, contribute more than 17 percent of Russia's electricity, and HEP is the main non-

fossil fuel source of electricity. The other is nuclear power, which accounts for more than 16 percent of Russia's electricity production. Russia has 31 nuclear reactors, all of them in European Russia. Its safety record remains good, although 15 of these power stations have fewer than 10 years remaining of their planned 30-year lives, and most use the same design that failed disasterously at Chernobyl (in Ukraine) in 1986. By 2010, the Russian Ministry of

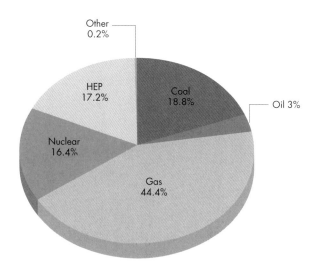

▲ Electricity production by type

▼ A coal miner stands near industrial facilities in the Siberian city of Novokuznetsk, one of many mining and industrial cities that sprang up in the Stalin era.

▶ Nickel is smelted in the Siberian city of Norilsk. Nickel is one of Russia's main nonenergy mineral resources. Smelting nickel produces large amounts of toxic dust and pollution. Arctic winds carry pollution from Russian smelters like this as far as Canada and Scandinavia.

Atomic Energy intends to build new production units at five of the existing sites and aims to have doubled nuclear electricity production by 2020.

NONENERGY RESOURCES

Russia has some of the world's largest deposits of minerals, including iron and nickel ores, gold, diamonds, and many nonferrous metals and nonmetallic minerals. However, many of these are difficult to extract because they are in remote areas with very hostile climates. In spite of this, Russia is still a leading producer of various minerals. In 2003, the country accounted for 22 percent of the world's nickel production, 16 percent of its diamonds, about 7 percent of its gold, and about 7 percent of its iron ore.

 Did You Know?

The iron ore deposits in the Kursk Magnetic Anomaly, located close to the Ukrainian border in the southwest of Russia, are believed to contain one-sixth of the world's total reserves.

Focus on: Russian Forestry

About 22 percent of the world's forests and 50 percent of its coniferous forests are in Russia. Russia's forests cover an area larger than the continental United States. Of Russia's 1.88 billion acres (764 million hectares) of forests, 78 percent are in Siberia and the far east of the country. Only 55 percent of this forested area is of commercial value, and access to it is difficult because more than half of Russian forests grow on permafrost soils unsuitable for road or rail. As a result, Russia currently accounts for only 3 percent of the world's timber production, and much of this is in the form of lumber (rough sawn wood) rather than the more profitable processed timber.

CHAPTER 7

Economy and Income

In 2004, Russia's economy grew by about 7 percent—faster than any of the world's other leading industrial powers. 2004 was also the sixth year in a row that the country's economy had grown, mainly as the result of high world oil prices and increasing global demand for Russian energy exports.

ENERGY DEPENDENCY

Russia's heavy dependence on energy exports means that its economy is especially vulnerable to changes in world oil prices. It has been estimated that a U.S.$1 change in the price of a barrel of oil equates to a U.S.$1.4 billion change in Russian revenues. Since the year 2000, high oil prices (brought about mainly by conflict and instability in the oil-rich Gulf region of the Middle East) have given Russia record levels of oil earnings. In recognition of this windfall, Russia's government established a stabilization fund in January 2004. This will enable Russia to store some of its oil profits to guard against any future downturn in the price of oil and, therefore, the country's economy. By the end of 2005, the stabilization fund was estimated to be worth around U.S.$52 billion—equivalent to approximately 7 percent of Russia's annual income in the same year. The country's government is under political pressure to spend some of this fund in order to quickly improve social conditions such as housing and health care, but financial experts warn that injecting so much money into these areas could lead to high inflation and damage to Russia's economy.

KEEPING A BALANCE

Russia's "petrodollar boom" follows a decade of economic turmoil. During the Soviet era, nearly all aspects of the economy were centrally planned and controlled. After the collapse of the Soviet Union, the planned economy was scrapped, and Russia started to adopt a broadly free-market capitalist economy, like those of the United States, Japan, and Europe. Economic

◀ This building in Moscow is the headquarters of the energy company Gazprom, the largest company in Russia. Gazprom produces about 8 percent of Russia's GDP. It is quickly becoming one of the largest companies in the world.

reforms had begun even before the end of the Soviet Union, but they did not do enough and came too late. Industrial and agricultural output fell sharply in 1990–1991. Russia's annual income in 1991 was more than 20 percent lower than it had been in 1989, and its economy entered a five-year period of virtual collapse. People waited in long lines for even the most basic foodstuffs and industrial goods. By the mid-1990s, there were signs of a recovery, as private businesses and foreign investors began to buy into the economy. People's standard of living improved, but the recovery was short-lived. A financial crisis that began in Asia in 1997 spread to Russia and led many investors to withdraw from the Russian economy. The country's government was forced to devalue the Russian currency to improve its competitiveness, but Russia's economy and living standards had already deteriorated. By 2000, Russia's economy had shrunk to its 1960 level. The petrodollar boom has since brought rapid economic growth to the country, but analysts believe that a collapse in oil prices would be mirrored in Russia's economy and that Russia has yet to enter a period of secure economic growth.

▲ The TsUM shopping mall in Moscow has been extensively refurbished. It is one of the largest and most successful of the many retail centers in Russia.

Economic Data

🗀 Gross National Income (GNI) in U.S.$: 639,080,000,000

🗀 World rank by GNI: 15

🗀 GNI per capita in U.S.$: 4,460

🗀 World rank by GNI per capita: 90

🗀 Economic growth: 7.0%

Source: World Bank

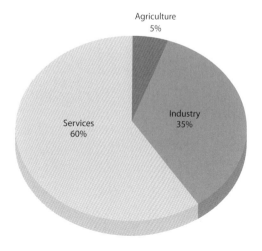

Agriculture 5%

Industry 35%

Services 60%

▲ Contribution by sector to national income

ECONOMIC STRUCTURE

Besides the energy and minerals sectors, Russia's economy is based upon a balance of other industries, including manufacturing and heavy industry, services, and agriculture. The service sector, which includes banking, insurance, and retail, has expanded very quickly as Russia's internal market has developed. Consumer demand, an important indicator of this growth, increased by more than 12 percent a year between 2000 and 2005. In 1989, services accounted for only 33 percent of Russia's GDP. By 2003, services had increased to become the largest sector of the country's economy.

The industrial sector dominated Russia during the Soviet era and still accounted for 50 percent of GDP in 1989, but by 2003, this had fallen to 35 percent. A lack of investment during the Soviet era had left many industries inefficient and unable to compete in the new open, global market. Russia still has numerous industries, however, particularly metal fabrication, heavy

▲ In spite of the country's economic recovery, poverty remains a major problem in Russia. This elderly woman collects food from a distribution point for homeless people in Moscow in January 2006.

engineering, and chemicals. Agriculture has fallen from making up 17 percent of Russia's GDP in 1989 to just 5 percent in 2003. Like industry, agriculture has suffered from years of underinvestment and is still adjusting to the highly competitive global food markets. After decline in the 1990s, favorable weather conditions during the period between 2001 and 2006 resulted in good yields of Russia's

 Did You Know?

In 1990, the U.S. restaurant chain McDonald's became one of the first companies to take advantage of Russia's economic reforms when it opened a restaurant in Moscow. By 2006, McDonald's had 103 outlets in Russia, serving about 200,000 people per day.

agricultural staples—wheat, barley, and corn. In spite of this, the poor condition of Russia's farm machinery and continued restructuring of the entire farming sector mean that the contribution of agriculture to the country's GDP is unlikely to increase in the foreseeable future.

? Did You Know?

In 1994, there were just four U.S.$ billionaires in Russia. Today, there are 36—more than in Britain, France, or Japan.

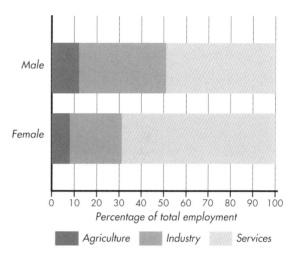

▲ Labor force by sector and gender

Focus on: Poverty and the New Billionaires

Russia's economic transformation has caused considerable hardship for many ordinary Russian people. Russia now has higher unemployment and greater poverty than it did at the end of the Soviet era, and it has periodic shortages of supplies. In 2004, official government figures put the number of people in Russia living in poverty at about 25.5 million, or 18 percent of the population. Some individuals have benefited greatly, however, particularly those who purchased parts of the former Soviet energy industry. Roman Abramovich is one such individual. In 2005, Abramovich was listed as the world's twenty-first wealthiest person and the wealthiest Russian, with a personal fortune of U.S.$13.3 billion. Besides oil, he has interests in politics and sports, owning a Russian hockey team and the Chelsea Football Club, a leading British soccer team. Newly superrich people in Russia can assert great political influence, and this has occasionally bought them into conflict with President Putin.

► Russian businessman Boris Berezovsky stands outside Russia's embassy in London, England, in 2004. He was protesting the arrest for tax evasion of Russian billionairre Mikhail Khodorkovsky, head of the Yukos, an oil company.

CHAPTER 8

Global Connections

Following the breakup of the Soviet Union, the new Russia was forced to come to terms with the fact that it was no longer one of the world's superpowers. Today, Russia is redefining its global relations and realigning itself internationally.

THE COLD WAR ERA

In the aftermath of World War II, the Soviet Union and the United States emerged as the world's two superpowers. However, these superpowers had very different political outlooks and considered each other a serious threat. The weapons of the Cold War were technological advancement, displays of military might, and political propaganda. The countries competed in an arms race to develop ever more destructive and further-reaching weapons, and a space race in which each side sought to outdo the other's latest technological achievements.

Although the United States and the Soviet Union were never directly at war with each another, they engaged in numerous conflicts by supporting opposing regimes in other parts of the world with weapons, funds, and military advice. The Korean War (1950–1953) and the Vietnam War (1954–1975) are the clearest examples of this type of conflict. Other wars, such as that in Afghanistan (1979–1989), were also affected.

MOVING FORWARD

The collapse of the Soviet Union in late 1991 signaled the end of the Cold War. Russia was the largest and most significant of the countries to emerge from the Soviet Union and has been renegotiating its global relationships ever since. Russia's most important global connections are with Europe, China, Central Asia, the United States, and Japan.

◄ Russian soldiers march at a Victory Day parade in May 2006. This event celebrates the historic Soviet victory in World War II. Russia's army is one of the world's largest military forces.

The majority of Russia's people live in its western regions bordering Europe. This area is the focus of much of Russia's trade. The European Union (EU) is a powerful and wealthy trading group. The EU expanded in 2004 to absorb the former Soviet countries of Estonia, Latvia, and Lithuania. Bulgaria and Romania both have a history of strong political and economic ties with Russia (and, before that, the Soviet Union); they joined the EU in 2007. These political shifts challenge Russia's influence in the region, but Russia's large reserves of natural resources means that the EU is also heavily dependent on Russia.

► A photo from 1961 shows U.S. soldiers in a tank near one of the checkpoints at the Berlin Wall, a symbol of the Cold War era. A sign in English, Russian, French, and German warns: "You are leaving the American sector" of Berlin.

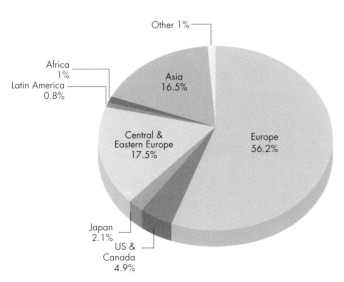

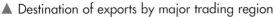
▲ Destination of exports by major trading region

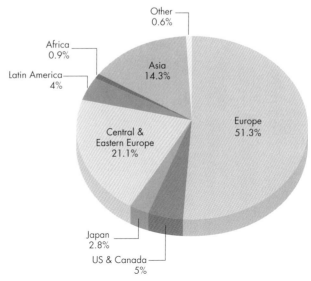
▲ Origin of imports by major trading region

To the east, Russia is geographically close to the fast-growing economies of China and South Korea and the more established economy of Japan. This region of Asia, and particularly China, is becoming an important center of the global economy, challenging the strength of the EU and the United States. Russia is building strong relationships in this region, constructing oil pipelines from Siberia to supply China and Japan in return for greater Chinese and Japanese investment in the Russian economy. Russia's relationship with China is particularly significant. In 2001 the two countries signed the Treaty for Good Neighborliness, Friendship, and Cooperation as a symbol of their close ties. By August 2005, cooperation between Russia and China had extended into defense, as their forces engaged in Peace Mission 2005. their first joint military exercises.

▼ Chinese marine vehicles land during Peace Mission 2005, joint military exercises held by Russia and China in August 2005. Peace Mission 2005 aimed to deepen mutual trust, promote friendship, and enhance cooperation between the two nations.

Some political experts believe that the closer ties between Russia and China are a response to the dominant influence of the United States in world affairs. Russia, however, maintains that its relationship with the United States is just as important. The United States is a major trading partner for Russia, and the two countries also cooperate in areas such as space exploration.

More recently, Russia and the United States have worked together in the global fight against terrorism, following terrorist attacks on the United States on September 11, 2001, and by Chechen separatists in Russia. Chechen terrorist attacks included hostage sieges in a Moscow theater in 2002 and in a school in Beslan in 2004. In spite of being united in their desire to defeat terrorism, Russia and the United States do not always agree. In 2003, the United States and its allies (including Britain) invaded Iraq to overthrow the regime of Saddam Hussein. They claimed that Saddam's government was supporting terrorist activity. Russia joined with France and Germany to criticize the invasion and argue for a diplomatic solution.

WORLD INFLUENCE

Russia plays an influential role in global politics because of the position it inherited from the Soviet Union as one of the five permanent members of the UN Security Council, the body responsible for overseeing global peace and security. In 1998, Russia gained further global stature when it joined the G7 group of leading industrialized economies to form the new G8. The G8 group meets annually to discuss global issues of mutual interest such as trade, poverty, and security. In 2006, Russia held the presidency of the G8 for the first time, and the annual G8 summit was held in St. Petersburg.

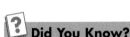

Did You Know?

During the Cold War era, the Soviet army was the largest active army in the world, with between 3 million and 5 million soldiers.

Did You Know?

In the 1992 Olympic Games, athletes belonging to countries of the CIS (see below) competed as a single unified team. CIS countries have since competed individually.

▲ One of the major peace missions for Russian forces in recent years was their deployment in Kosovo as part of a NATO force. This soldier (left) is part of a security escort for Serb children on their way to school in December 1999.

Focus on: The Commonwealth of Independent States

The Commonwealth of Independent States (CIS) was created in December 1991 out of the breakup of the Soviet Union. It is an alliance—similar to the European Union—of 11 of the 15 former Soviet republics: Armenia, Azerbaijan, Belarus, Georgia, Kazakhstan, Kyrgyzstan, Moldova, Russia, Tajikistan, Ukraine, and Uzbekistan. (Turkmenistan is an associate member, having withdrawn from permanent membership in 2005.) The CIS member countries cooperate on issues such as economics, security, and foreign policy. In particular, they aim to establish a free trade zone similar to that of the European Union. Since 2003, political changes have brought several CIS member countries closer with Europe and less close with the CIS and Russia, its dominant nation. Some political experts question whether the CIS will continue to exist. All of them agree, however, that Russia, as the group's largest and most politically important country, will play a vital role in determining the future of the CIS.

CHAPTER 9

Transportation and Communications

Transportation and communications systems are vital to a country of Russia's size. Following the breakup of the Soviet Union, Russia inherited much of its huge transportation and communications network. Since then, Russia has worked to create new systems that meet its present needs.

RAILWAYS

With 54,159 miles (87,157 km) of track, Russia's rail network is second in length only to the rail network of the United States. Russia's railways are well connected to the 15 republics of the former Soviet Union, because they were once part of the much larger Soviet rail network. In 1998, Russia's government began to reform the network in a process that led, in September 2003, to the formation of a new public corporation, Russian Railways (RZD). The new structure opened up possibilities for greater investment in the railways. For example, it allowed private operators to run trains on the existing network. It is too early to assess the full impact of the reforms, but Russia's rail system remains vital to its economy.

AIR TRAVEL

Because of its vast size, Russia has made use of aviation as a means of transportation for many years. Its national airline was founded under the Soviets in 1923. In 1932, this airline was named Aeroflot and went on to become a

▼ A platform full of passengers greets a train on the Trans-Siberian Railway, one of the longest rail routes in the world. It takes seven days to complete!

104

pioneer in civil aviation. Aeroflot established the world's first passenger jet services in 1956. Following the collapse of the Soviet Union, Aeroflot was split into various national airlines to serve the newly independent states. The name Aeroflot was kept and used by the new Russian national air carrier. Aeroflot flies regular routes to 89 cities in 47 countries and has partnerships with other international airlines to extend their services. Of the 89 cities served by Aeroflot, 25 of them are within Russia, which makes it Russia's main carrier for both domestic and international flights.

▲ Passengers disembark from an Aeroflot aircraft at Riga International Airport in Latvia. Many of Aeroflot's busiest routes are within Russia or connect Russia to other former Soviet republics.

Transport & Communications Data

- 🗁 Total roads: 333,871 miles/537,289 km
- 🗁 Total paved roads: 225,029 miles/ 362,133 km
- 🗁 Total unpaved roads: 108,842 miles/ 175,156 km
- 🗁 Total railways: 54,159 miles/87,157 km
- 🗁 Airports: 1,623
- 🗁 Cars per 1,000 people: 140
- 🗁 Cellular phones per 1,000 people: 517
- 🗁 Personal computers per 1,000 people: 132
- 🗁 Internet users per 1,000 people: 111

Source: World Bank and CIA World Factbook

Did You Know?

Russia's railways carry more freight than any other railways in the world, except for those in China and the United States. For passenger travel, Russia's railways rank fourth in the world, behind China, India, and Japan.

WATERWAYS

Russia's navigable waterways cover about 59,650 miles (96,000 km) and are second only to China's in their extent. They provide important routes for the importing and exporting of freight as well as for movement within Russia. The country's most important waterways are a system of about 44,740 miles (72,000 km) in European Russia that connect the Baltic Sea, White Sea, Caspian Sea, Sea of Azov, and Black Sea. In 2002, Russia signed an agreement to become part of a growing European inland waterway network that extends from the Atlantic Ocean, in the west, to the Ural Mountains, in the east. It connects 37 countries and incorporates about 350 major ports.

MEDIA AND TELECOMMUNICATIONS

During the Soviet era, telecommunications and the media were heavily controlled by the state. Post-Soviet Russia has seen this change radically, with greater freedom of the media (television, radio, and press) and a proliferation of new communications technologies, such as cellular phones, e-mail, and the Internet.

The transition to an open and free media has not been smooth, however. In recent times, Russia's government has actually increased its control of the major media channels. For example, in 2002 the general manager of the NTV channel was fired for its coverage of the Moscow theater siege because the channel's method of reporting angered President Putin. In 2005, Russia Today, a satellite news channel reporting global affairs news in English but from a Russian perspective, was launched. This channel is funded and controlled by Russia's government.

During the Soviet era, Russia's landline telephone network was largely confined to the needs of the government and the military. Following the collapse of the Soviet Union, it was anticipated that Russia's landline network

◀ A cargo vessel on the Volga River near St. Petersburg. The Volga is one of Russia's most important of navigable waterways.

Focus on: The Russian Underground

During the Soviet era, the government declared that any city of more than one million people should have an underground rail system, or subway. As a result, six Russian cities have subway systems, with a further six planned or under construction. In 2005, the overall length of functioning subway lines was 261 miles (420 km), with 267 stations and an annual passenger capacity of more than 4 billion. Tickets are inexpensive and trains are frequent and efficient. The most famous of the Russian subway systems is in Moscow. Its first 7.5-mile (12-km) line was opened in 1935, and the subway has since expanded to 12 lines, 165 stations, and more than 168 miles (270 km) of track. It is the world's busiest subway, carrying between 8 million and 9 million passengers every weekday, with trains arriving every 90 seconds during peak hours.

▶ Commuters pass through one of the ornately decorated tunnels at Arbatskaya Station on the Arbatsko-Pokrovskaya line of the Moscow subway.

would grow rapidly. In reality, its growth has been much slower than anticipated because of the high rates charged and the emergence of cellular networks as an alternative. By 2005, only about 30 percent of the population were connected to the landline telephone network. In contrast, Russia's cellular network has grown rapidly. By 2005, it was estimated to have reached 52 percent of the country's population, up from just 5 percent in 2001. Internet use has also grown rapidly in Russia, with about 13 percent of the population having Internet access by 2005, an increase from only 3 percent in 2001.

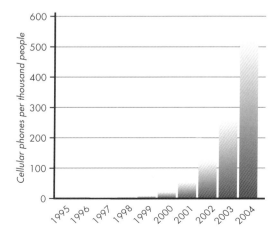

▲ Cellular phone use, 1995–2004

CHAPTER 10

Education and Health

Under Soviet control, education and health care were wholly funded by the state and available to all. The education system was rigid and standardized, but it was of high quality and it helped the Soviet Union become a world leader in science and technology. Health care was also of a high standard, with one of the best patient-to-doctor ratios in the world. Russia inherited these systems but has found them difficult to maintain.

EDUCATION

High value is placed on education in Russia, and discipline and attendance in schools are good. Most students remain within the state-funded education system, but private schools and special foreign language and international schools are now available for those able to afford them. Curriculum and examination procedures are being reviewed, and the Soviet style of rote teaching is being replaced by approaches that encourage problem-solving and creative thinking. An example of these reforms is the introduction of greater specialization for 16- to 18-year-olds. Under new proposals, these students will specialize in four or five subjects rather than the 12 or even 14 currently studied.

Education and Health Data

- Life expectancy at birth, male: 58.8
- Life expectancy at birth, female: 72
- Infant mortality rate per 1,000: 16
- Under five mortality rate per 1,000: 21
- Physicians per 1,000 people: 4.3
- Health expenditure as % of GDP: 5.6%
- Education expenditure as % of GDP: 3.7%
- Primary school net enrollment: 93%
- Student-teacher ratio, primary: 16.6
- Adult literacy as % age 15+: 99.4

Source: United Nations Agencies and World Bank

◀ Children play outside their school in the village of Bol'shoye Goloustnoye in Siberia, close to Lake Baikal. Recruiting teachers to work in such remote locations is just one of the challenges facing Russia's education system.

▲ Schools equipped with new technology can offer a high-quality education equivalent to that in Europe or the United States, but providing such technology to all Russian schools is very expensive.

Reform is not easy, however, with more than 63,000 schools and many staff who were themselves educated and trained under the Soviet system. Recruiting new teachers into state schools is also problematic, because salaries are relatively low. English and information technology (IT) teachers, for example, can earn higher incomes working for foreign-language schools or businesses. The government is trying to address the problem with large increases in teachers' salaries.

HEALTH CARE

Russia has not been able to maintain the high standards of its health-care system in the post-Soviet era, and the health of its population has suffered as a result. Life expectancy at birth, for example, fell from 68 years in 1991 to 65.4 years in 2003 (compared to 77 years in the United States and 78 years in Britain). Not all trends are negative, however, and some basic health-care indicators have improved since 1991. Child immunization rates have increased from about 77 percent to 97 percent, and infant mortality (the number of children dying before the age of one year) fell from 21 per 1,000 live births in 1991 to 16 per 1,000 live births by 2003.

UNDER PRESSURE

Of great concern is the increase in illnesses and deaths related to habits such as drinking and smoking. Alcoholism, especially among men, is a particular problem in Russia, and it is causing high levels of death from accidents and an increase in conditions such as heart and liver disease. Russia has among the highest number of smokers in the world; in 2005, 36 percent of Russia's adults and 62 percent of its adult men were smokers. Smoking has increased rapidly among Russia's women in recent years—particularly young, urban women—rising from

Focus on: Higher Education

During the Soviet era, higher education was state-funded and students were paid a small state grant during their studies. They were also guaranteed a job upon graduation, though this was centrally allocated and could be very distant from their hometown. Higher education is still state-funded and desirable for many young people. Competition for places is intense and, as a result, some universities now supplement their state-funded places with additional fee-paying places. There are 48 universities in Russia and more than 500 higher education institutions (some of them private) with a total of about 3 million students between them.

▲ Students at Moscow State University, one of the most prestigious higher education institutes in the country.

10 percent of adult women in 1994 to 15 percent by 2005.

The increase in diseases related to habits such as smoking and drinking alcohol is placing additional pressure on Russia's already

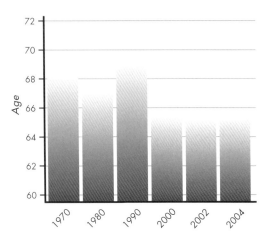

▲ Life expectancy at birth, 1970–2004

overstretched health-care system. Many of the country's health-care facilities are in need of modernization, and staff shortages as a result of poor pay and working conditions are becoming more common. In addition, large variations in health-care quality are emerging between the regions. In response to these changes, private health care is expanding rapidly and attracting many medical professionals away from the state system by offering better opportunities and higher pay.

Since the collapse of the Soviet Union, an HIV/AIDS epidemic has begun in Russia. Experts fear it could quickly spread out of control if urgent action is not taken. By the end of 2004, there were 300,000 officially registered cases of HIV, but because of underreporting, the real level is estimated to be as high as

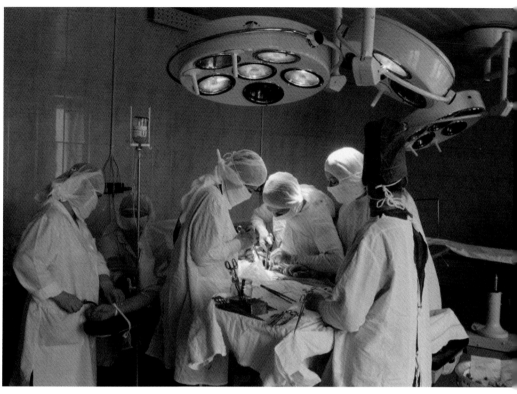

► Surgeons perform an operation in a hospital in the Siberian city of Irkutsk. Although Russia has some highly skilled medical staff, many Russian doctors and nurses leave the country because they can earn more money working outside Russia.

1.4 million people living with HIV. The majority (about 80 percent) of HIV cases are related to drug abuse and the use of infected needles. Sexual transmission (increasingly through prostitution) accounts for the balance of cases. HIV incidence is particularly high among Russia's youth (15- to 29-year-olds), who account for three-quarters of reported new cases. The government seems unable to cope with the scale of the problem, providing only 10 percent of patients with the anti-retroviral drugs needed to delay the onset of AIDS. Needle exchange services and public education programs are being used to try to halt the epidemic, but many experts believe it will get much worse before it gets better.

Focus on: Tuberculosis

Russia has one of the highest rates of tuberculosis (TB) in the world, with more than 121,000 new cases identified in 2004. TB is particularly widespread among the prison population, but it is also prevalent in the population at large. The poor availability of drugs, together with increasingly drug-resistant forms of TB, has prolonged and extended the spread of TB to almost epidemic proportions. Russia is now engaged in a global strategy to combat the further spread of the disease through a World Health Organization program.

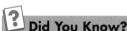 **Did You Know?**

In 2002, Russia's production and consumption of cigarettes was equivalent to six cigarettes per day for every single person. Smoking-related diseases kill 270,00 people each year in Russia—more than AIDS, road accidents, drug abuse, murder, and suicide put together.

CHAPTER 11

Culture and Religion

Russian culture and religion are heavily influenced by the political transitions of the country's history. During the Soviet era, for example, the Communist government demanded that all art must serve the interests of the state and the Communist Party, and religion was suppressed in favor of a state policy of atheism. Today, culture and religion in Russia enjoy much greater freedoms and also a higher degree of external influence.

PRE-SOVIET CULTURE

During the nineteenth and early twentieth centuries, before the founding of the Communist state, Russia went through an era in which many of the country's most famous cultural contributors were producing their works. These included poet and writer Alexander Pushkin (1799–1837), whose poetry continues to be popular among many Russians today.

In the mid-nineteenth century, the novels of Leo Tolstoy (1828–1910), which included *War and Peace* (1869) and *Anna Karenina* (1877), made a significant contribution to Russian literature. Another important writer during this period was Fyodor Dostoevsky (1821–1881), whose works included *Crime and Punishment* (1866), *The Idiot* (1869), and *The Brothers Karamazov* (1869). Tolstoy and Dostoevsky are widely recognized as being among the world's literary greats. Another famous Russian writer is Anton Chekhov (1860–1904), who is best known for plays such as *The Three Sisters* (1901) and *The Cherry Orchard* (1904) and also wrote many short stories.

Several of Russia's most famous composers were also active during the pre-Communist era. They included Nikolay Rimsky-Korsakov (1844–1908) and Alexander Borodin (1833–1887), who were known for their operatic works but who also wrote a wide range of

◀ Dmitri Gudanov, a dancer with the Bolshoi Ballet, performs in *Swan Lake* at the Royal Opera House in London, England, in August 2006. The Bolshoi is Russia's most famous ballet company.

Focus on: Alexander Solzhenitsyn

One of the best-known writers who was persecuted during the Soviet era is Alexander Solzhenitsyn (1918–). Solzhenitsyn first fell foul of the Soviet regime when he wrote a letter criticizing Stalin shortly after World War II. He was sentenced to eight years in prison and labor camps. This harsh experience became the basis for Solzhenitsyn's first published work, *One Day in the Life of Ivan Denisovich* (1962), which was at first well received in the post-Stalin USSR. As his writing became openly critical of the government of the day, however, Solzhenitsyn found his works banned and resorted to publishing abroad or to samizdat, or illegal self-publishing. Solzhenitsyn was awarded the Nobel Prize for Literature in 1970 but was unable to claim it for fear of not being allowed to return to the USSR. Three years later, in 1973, his book *The Gulag Archipelago* looked at the extensive Russian prison system, and it led to Solzhenitsyn being arrested for treason. He was deported in February 1974. It was not until the policy of glasnost was introduced in the late 1980s that Solzhenitsyn's work was published again in the USSR. In 1990, Solzhenitsyn's Soviet citizenship was restored, and he eventually returned to Russia in 1994.

▶ The great writer Alexander Solzhenitsyn enjoys a walk shortly after his return to Russia in 1994.

music based on traditional Russian themes. The most significant composer of this time, however, was Pyotr Tchaikovsky (1840–1893), who became the first Russian composer to attract major attention from outside his home country. Some of his most famous works include the opera *Eugene Onegin* (1879), the ballet *The Nutcracker* (1892), and grand orchestral pieces such as *Romeo and Juliet* (1870).

Under the Soviet system, many of the literary and musical traditions of pre-Communist Russia continued, but a large number of artists and writers felt the need to emigrate in order to have creative freedom. Under Stalin's "Socialist Realism" policies, all art forms were required to serve the interests of the USSR. Much of the cultural output during this period was mundane and of limited interest, but exceptions exist. In literature, authors such as Boris Pasternak (1890–1960) and Alexander Solzhenitsyn continued to produce strong novels. In classical music, Dmitry Shostakovich (1906–1975) and Sergei Rachmaninov (1873–1943) made significant contributions.

POST-SOVIET CULTURE

Since the political transformations of 1991, Russians have become very interested in reexamining their pre-Soviet culture and elements of the Soviet era itself. This interest is motivated by a desire to regain aspects of Russia's cultural heritage. Russian artists and writers, such as Alexander Solzhenitsyn, whose works were shunned or even banned during the Soviet era, are now finding new audiences and recognition. There is also a wealth of new influences as Russia's culture, like all other aspects of life, is affected by the opening up of Russia to wider global forces. Film, music, art, and literature from outside Russia bring new experiences, not just for audiences but also for Russian artists, who now enjoy complete artistic freedom and are limited only by what consumers will buy.

RELIGION

Since Russia was converted in 988, the official state religion has been Orthodox Christianity. In the fifteenth century, the Russian Orthodox Church emerged as a form of orthodoxy that was distinct from the broader Eastern Orthodox Church. The Soviet era ushered in changes, as the Church was separated from the state and the Soviet Union became officially atheist. The Communist government, particularly under Stalin, tried to suppress religion in the belief that it was incompatible with the ideals of the Communist Party. Possessions from the Orthodox Church were seized, and many churches and cathedrals were destroyed.

In 1985, this suppression of religion was relaxed and, in 1990, new laws guaranteeing religious freedom came into force. Christianity, and specifically Orthodox Christianity, remains the largest religion in Russia today, although several other forms of Christianity are now becoming popular in the country. Russia's other main religions are Islam and Judaism. Many Russian Jews emigrated to Israel following the collapse of the Soviet Union and the subsequent removal of travel restrictions. Today, Jews in Russia make up a small minority—about 0.4 percent—of the population. Islam is more popular, with almost 8 percent of the country's

◀ During Christmas ceremonies, Russian girls light candles in a church in the village of Zhilino, about 12.5 miles (20 km) outside Moscow. The Russian Orthodox Church celebrates Christmas on January 7.

population following it, but it is heavily concentrated in central and southern regions of the country. Some Islamist factions have been linked to the troubled south of Russia, where there is an ongoing struggle by some regions, particularly Chechnya, for independence from Russia. Islamic militant groups have been blamed for numerous acts of terrorism against Russian civilians and accused of having links with organizations such as al-Qaeda.

▲ The Great Mosque, located in the city of Kazan, was destroyed by Ivan the Terrible. It was rebuilt in 1996 with the aid of funds from Saudi Arabia. It is the largest mosque in Russia.

❓ Did You Know?

Before the Russian Revolution, there were 54,000 functioning parishes and more than 150 bishops in Russia. By 1939, the country had fewer than 100 functioning parishes and only four bishops. Today, Russia has more than 23,000 parishes and 154 bishops.

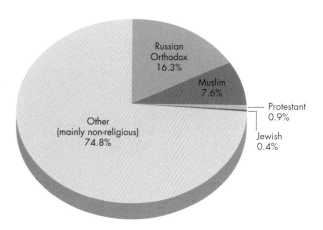

Russian Orthodox 16.3%
Muslim 7.6%
Protestant 0.9%
Jewish 0.4%
Other (mainly non-religious) 74.8%

▲ Major religions

CHAPTER 12

Leisure and Tourism

During the Soviet era, leisure was a state-sponsored activity. Sports facilities, theaters, movies, galleries, and museums were all subsidized by the state, providing universal access for little or no payment. Tourism within the country was very underdeveloped, although the number of resorts, sanatoriums, hotels, and other tourist facilities grew gradually over time. A special passport was needed for foreign trips, and this was only issued to the most privileged members of the Communist Party. In post-Soviet Russia, the situation is dramatically different.

RUSSIAN TOURISTS ABROAD

Restrictions on foreign travel were relaxed soon after the collapse of the Soviet Union. Since then, rising living standards have enabled many Russians to take vacations abroad. Among the most popular countries visited by Russians are Turkey, France, Germany, Egypt, and Poland, all of which allow free (nonvisa) passage for Russian passport holders. President Putin is working with other European countries to remove visa requirements and encourage greater travel between Russia and Europe. Beyond Europe, destinations in Asia such as Vietnam and Thailand are increasingly popular with Russians.

TOURISM IN RUSSIA

The number of foreign tourists visiting Russia grew dramatically in the years following the end of the Soviet era. Tourist numbers reached 10 million visitors per year by 1995, reached just short of 19 million in 1999, and peaked at more than 23 million in 2002 before dropping slightly. One-quarter of all visitors to Russia head for Moscow, drawn by the city's numerous attractions, which include Red Square, the

◄ Tourists stroll in the plaza in front of the Winter Palace in St. Petersburg. Built between 1754 and 1762, this palace was once home to czars. It is now best known as part of the world-famous Hermitage Museum.

▲ Winter sports enthusiasts enjoy skiing on Mount Cheget in the Caucasus Mountains.

Kremlin buildings, and Lenin's mausoleum. St. Petersburg is another favorite destination, famous for its impressive architecture and its cultural attractions. These attractions include the Hermitage Museum that, with more than three million items, houses one of the largest and most important art collections in the world. Beyond the appeal of the so-called "twin capitals" of Moscow and St. Petersburg, tourists flock to the coastal resorts around the Black Sea and, in winter, to the ski resorts in the Caucasus and Ural Mountains.

With tourism set to become the world's biggest industry during the twenty-first century, Russia is eager to share in the potential benefits. The country offers many possibilities for tourist activities, and Russian entrepreneurs have been quick to exploit outside interest. The most extreme example of this is space tourism! Some foreign citizens are willing to pay U.S.$20 million and train for months for the chance to become one of the growing number of "space tourists" who have traveled to the International Space Station on a Russian rocket. In 2001, Denis Tito from the United States became the first space tourist. By 2007, three others had followed him. Tourist places on Russian space missions are now fully booked until 2009.

SPORTS

During the Soviet period, the Communist Party considered success in sports at a global level as proof of its superiority. Soccer is the most popular sport in Russia and has many fans. In the 2004–2005 season, CSKA Moskva (Moscow) won the UEFA (Union of European Football Associations) Cup, one of Europe's most prestigious soccer competitions. CSKA was the first Russian team to win this tournament. Other popular sports in Russia include track and field, gymnastics, and tennis, and Russia has achieved international success in all of these. In tennis, Russia has produced a number of young stars, including the men Yevgeny Kafelnikov and Nikolay Davydenko and the women Maria Sharapova—the winner of the 2004 Wimbledon title—and Anna Kournikova.

Russia's climate means that winter sports are also popular, and Russia (previously as the USSR) has long been one of the world's dominant nations in figure skating and ice hockey. In recent times, however, this dominance has been reduced. It has been suggested that reasons for this are a reduction in the level of spending on sports by the government and the closure of many sporting facilities. The result has been that there is less opportunity for people, particularly the young, to participate in sports. Many private health and leisure facilities have opened to meet the needs of Russia's growing middle classes, but such places are expensive and beyond the reach of most Russians. In 2005, Russia's government announced a program to build more than 4,000 new sports facilities between 2006 and 2015. President Putin said the aim was to make sports facilities and healthy living available to as many people as possible. More than half of the new facilities will be targeted at children and young people. With these users in mind, many of the new facilities are being built alongside schools or higher education institutions.

Did You Know?

In the March 2006 world tennis rankings, six Russian women placed in the top twenty—more than from any other country, and twice the number of the next best country, France.

LEISURE

Modern Russians enjoy the same broad range of leisure activities as people in any country in the developed world. Western popular culture used to be banned in the USSR, but people are now free to have the same interests, watch the same films, and listen to the same music as their counterparts in the West. The Internet is increasingly popular and accessible in Russia. There are many talented and innovative

◀ The frozen surface of the Angara River in Irkutsk provides a group of boys with the chance for an informal game of ice hockey. Russia is among the world's most successful nations in this fast-moving winter sport.

Russians working in information technology (IT), enabling the country to make rapid progress in catching up after the years of Soviet isolation.

Russians love chess, and Russia has produced many of the world's best players. The title "Grandmaster" in chess was first formally conferred by Czar Nicholas II, who, in 1914, awarded it to five players who were finalists in a tournament in St. Petersburg.

Focus on: Dacha

A specifically Russian way of spending leisure time is to visit a dacha. A dacha is a vacation or summer house that many Russian families have in addition to an urban apartment. A dacha is always in the countryside, often near a lake or river, and can be anything from a modest wooden hut to an elaborate, brick house with a sauna, satellite dish, and central heating. Most often in the summer but sometimes in other seasons, Russians love to escape the bustle of city life to retreat for a weekend or longer to the clean air and the quiet of the country.

Tourism in Russia

- Tourist arrivals, millions: 22.051
- Earnings from tourism in U.S.$: 6,958,000,000
- Tourism as % foreign earnings: 3.4
- Tourist departures, millions: 24.410
- Expenditure on tourism in U.S.$: 16,527,000,000

Source: World Bank

▲ A group of older men play chess on a park bench along Nevsky Prospekt, one of the main roads in St. Petersburg.

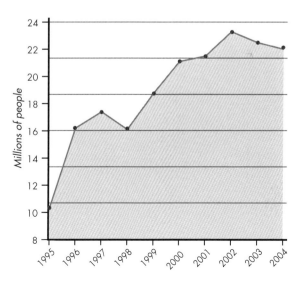

▲ Changes in international tourism, 1995–2004

CHAPTER 13

Environment and Conservation

With such a vast landscape, there are parts of Russia that are virtually untouched by human activity. In spite of this, Russia's environment is sometimes far from healthy and faces numerous challenges. Many of these challenges are associated with years of neglect under the Soviet administration.

THE SOVIET LEGACY

The policies of the Soviet era focused on rapid industrialization and economic growth, at almost any cost. For more than half a century, these policies allowed industrial, mining, and nuclear wastes, agricultural chemicals, and human waste (raw sewage) to be discharged freely into Russia's rivers and lakes. There was similar disregard for air quality, and Russia's air pollution by the industrial, energy, transportation, and domestic sectors was among the highest in the world. Studies completed in the late 1990s found that more than 200 Russian cities failed to meet nationally accepted guidelines (similar to those used in the United States and elsewhere). In eight cities—those associated with heavy industry, in particular—air quality was up to ten times worse than Russian health standards recommended.

During the economic downturn that followed the collapse of the Soviet Union, many of Russia's industries reduced production or closed altogether. This gave Russia's environment some short-term relief from pollutants and allowed some degree of recovery. The opening up of the economy, the desire for rapid economic growth, and higher personal incomes all brought new pressures, however. These pressures include the rapid increase in car ownership, which results in more air pollution. In 1991, Russia had roughly 87 vehicles for every 1,000 people; by 2001, it had risen to 176 vehicles per 1,000 people. In addition to these factors, there have been increased levels of consumption and the expansion of Russia's

◀ A heavily polluted forest near the Kolva River in the Usinsk region. This area has been contaminated by oil leaking into streams from corroded pipelines.

mining and energy industries. These new sources of pollution threaten to halt any decrease in pollution that resulted from industrial decline.

GROWING AWARENESS

Environmental awareness is growing in Russia, and the government recognizes that it can no longer ignore the environmental impacts of its policies. The cost of cleaning up decades of neglect is high, however, and the high number of demands for funding means that Russia's environmental budget is limited. Nevertheless, Russia has signaled its willingness to address the issues seriously. In November 2004, for example, Russia ratified the 1997 Kyoto Protocol, an agreement to reduce emissions of greenhouse gases by at least 5 percent of their 1990 levels by 2012. While the United States refuses to ratify the Kyoto Protocol, Russia's involvement, as the world's third biggest contributor of carbon dioxide, is vital. Russia should easily meet its Kyoto commitments; some estimate that Russia's emissions may be 20 percent below their 1990 levels already. Under a complex carbon trading agreement, Russia

could earn millions of dollars by selling its surplus allowances to those countries that are finding it harder to meet their commitments.

▲ Firemen spray a special foam that neutralizes oil spills on the surface of the Baltic Sea during a 2004 training exercise near the town of Baltiisk, in the Kaliningrad region. The exercise tested responses to a mass casualty and environmental disaster situation caused by a terrorist attack.

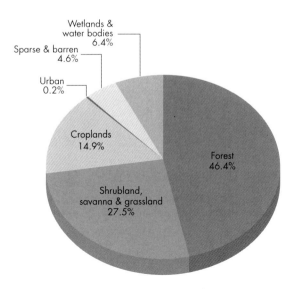

▲ Habitat type as a percentage of total area

 Did You Know?

Russia's government has estimated that poor air quality is a contributing factor to 17 percent of child illnesses and 10 percent of adult illnesses in the country.

POPULAR PRESSURE

Today, Russian people have greater access to information about the environment than in the past. They can now find out about worldwide environmental movements such as Greenpeace and Friends of the Earth. Greenpeace began operating in Russia in 1989. It has carried out campaigns on issues such as the protection of fragile habitats such as Lake Baikal, deforestation and replanting, and the safety and regulation of Russia's nuclear industry.

THE NUCLEAR CHALLENGE

One of the biggest threats to Russia's environment is from nuclear waste. Many of Russia's nuclear power stations are nearing the end of their operations and will need to be decommissioned, or shut down, in a process that generates vast amounts of highly radioactive waste. In addition to dealing with its own nuclear waste, Russia has also agreed to treat and store nuclear waste from other countries. The country's government believes it can do this safely and that by specializing in the handling of nuclear waste, it can also earn valuable foreign revenue. Campaign groups

such as Greenpeace are less convinced. They fear another nuclear accident such as the one that occurred at Chernobyl in 1986 that led to radioactive material being spread across a large part of northern Europe.

Environmental and Conservation Data

📂 Forested area as % total land area: 46.4

📂 Protected area as % total land area: 11.2

📂 Number of protected areas: 664

SPECIES DIVERSITY

Category	Known species	Threatened species
Mammals	90	14
Breeding birds	250	5
Reptiles	55	4
Amphibians	44	4
Fish	168	9
Plants	5,599	3

Source: World Resources Institute

◀ A Ukrainian woman lights a candle in memory of firemen who died fighting the disaster at the nuclear power plant in Chernobyl in 1986.

Another potential source of nuclear pollution in Russia comes from the decommissioning of naval submarines that were dumped off the north coast of the country during the Soviet era. There is concern that, over time, these submarines could leak radioactive materials into the northern seas and contaminate fish and other aquatic life.

Did You Know?

Russia has two unique species of large cat: the Amur tiger and the Amur leopard. Both are highly endangered. There are fewer than 40 Amur leopards left in the wild, and Amur tigers—the largest cats in the world— are thought to number fewer than 500.

▶ Crew members wait on board the new Gepard supersilent nuclear submarine. In spite of a series of accidents involving nuclear submarines and concerns over their safety, nuclear energy remains important to Russia's naval fleet.

Focus on: Lake Baikal

Lake Baikal is the deepest freshwater lake on Earth. It has 365 rivers flowing into it and only one river flowing out of it. Approximately half of the 2,615 plant and animal species found in the Baikal region are unique to the lake and its immediate surroundings. More than 560 species of algae and 52 species of fish live in Lake Baikal. The omul, an Arctic white fish that can only be found in Lake Baikal, accounts for two-thirds of the annual catch from the lake.

The most unique animal at Baikal is the freshwater seal known as the nerpa. The nerpa is also the only mammal to inhabit the lake. Scientists are unsure how a seal ended up in the middle of Asia when other members of its species all live in polar regions to the north. The favored theory is that the nerpa seals arrived in Lake Baikal during the last ice age when advancing polar ice pushed southward.

It is currently estimated that 60,000 nerpa live in Lake Baikal. Their population faces threats from hunting—about 3,500 young nerpa are killed each year for their skins—and from increased levels of pollutants in the water. One of the main sources of pollution is the Baikalsk pulp and paper plant, which has been pumping chlorine and other chemicals into the lake since 1966.

CHAPTER 14

Future Challenges

Looking ahead, the entire future of Russia presents a considerable challenge. It is a vast landmass to govern politically, especially when there are very real divides on the basis of ethnicity, religion, and quality of life. President Putin has introduced stringent reforms in an attempt to bring about a rapid improvement of Russia's economy and general living conditions, but many of his policies have encountered criticism. There is concern that too much power has been regained by the state and that the president, in particular, has excessive power. For example, several media networks have been closed down or nationalized, and many people say this has happened because these networks spoke out against Putin and the government of Russia.

The legacy of the Soviet era also remains apparent in many aspects of Russian life, such as the poor state of the country's environment. In places, the country's air, water, and soil pollution are among the worst in the world, and there is an urgent need to improve the regulation of future economic growth so that Russia's natural habitats are not further damaged. Health care and education are also in need of great attention to reverse the negative health trends of Russia's early post-Soviet era.

▼ An old woman begs for money from passersby on a cold street in Moscow. Resolving the enormous inequalities in wealth that have emerged since the breakup of the Soviet Union is one of the major challenges facing Russia.

▶ Russian soldiers patrol a street in Grozny, Chechnya. There has been tension and periodic violence between Russia and rebels who want an independent Chechnya. Overcoming the conflict in Chechnya is a major future challenge for Russia.

The Russian workforce also needs to adapt itself so that it is able to compete in an open and global economy.

Internationally, Russia is gaining considerable status. In 2006, it held the presidency of the G8, a group of the world's leading industrial nations, for the first time. Russia is also working toward becoming a member of the World Trade Organization (WTO), an international body that works to remove tariffs and other barriers to the free movement of capital, goods, and services between countries. Russia is forming strong political ties with China and Japan, both of which are keen to access its vast energy reserves. It also maintains important political ties with Europe and the United States.

If Russia continues to recover at its present rate, some experts believe it could quickly overtake Germany, France, and Britain to become the largest economy in Europe. Its energy reserves are certainly vital to this growth. But in order to maintain its recovery, Russia's economy will also need to diversify into other sectors. Russia needs to reward more than the small cluster of elite entrepreneurs who appear to have gained the most out of the country's recent transformation. Post-Soviet Russia is by no means free of the problems it inherited upon independence, and it has acquired several new problems. With signs of progress and some significant trials behind them, however, many Russians view the future with great optimism.

Time Line

2000 B.C. Early inhabitants settle in Russia.

c. 500 A.D. Slavs occupy much of eastern Europe and what is now Russia.

c. 850 Prince Rurik, a Viking trader, takes control of Slavs in Russia. Vikings form kingdom called Rus with its capital in Kiev (now in Ukraine).

c. 982 Christianity arrives in Russia through trade links with Constantinople (now Istanbul, Turkey); it becomes the state religion in 988.

c. 1237 Mongol Tatars led by Genghis Khan invade parts of Russia and gradually gain control of much of the country.

1447 Vasily II comes to power in Moscow and begins to consolidate his reign over other regions of Russia.

1613 Romanov family come to power in Russia and begins a period of rule that lasts until 1917.

1861 Czar Alexander II abolishes patterns of land ownership that have kept many Russians living as virtual serfs.

1881 Czar Alexander II is killed by revolutionary terrorists, but they fail to overthrow the monarchy.

1894 Czar Nicholas II comes to power following the death of his father, Czar Alexander III.

1915 Workers' strikes in protest of poor state of the economy.

1917 (January) Czar Nicholas II instructs the army to disperse strikers in Moscow who are calling for the abolition of the monarchy, but army refuses and joins the strikers.

1917 (February) Czar Nicholas II falls from power and flees to Tobolsk in northwestern Russia.

1917 (October) Under Vladimir Lenin, the Bolshevik Party leads a revolution against the provisional government.

1917–1921 Civil war between the Bolshevik Red Army of Lenin and the armies of the ousted provisional government; Bolsheviks win the war.

1922 The USSR (Union of Soviet Socialist Republics) is formed.

1924 Lenin's death results in a power struggle for control of the USSR.

1928 Joseph Stalin comes to power as leader of the USSR.

1941 German forces invade the USSR during World War II.

1945 At the end of World War II, political differences between the USSR and its allies (Britain, the United States, and France) lead to the Cold War.

1953 Joseph Stalin dies.

1957 USSR launches the first space satellite.

1961 USSR launches the first manned space flight.

1985 Mikhail Gorbachev becomes leader of the USSR and introduces reforms, including glasnost and perestroika.

1986 A nuclear reactor at Chernobyl (in Ukraine) explodes.

1991 (August) An attempted coup against Gorbachev is put down by President Boris Yeltsin.

1991 (December 25) Gorbachev resigns

1991 (December 31) The USSR ceases to exist.

1992 Russia emerges from the collapsed USSR with Yeltsin as its first president.

1994 Russia's army enters Chechnya to reclaim control of the breakaway republic.

1997 Ceasefire reached between Russia and Chechnya.

1998 Russia joins the G7 (the group of the world's seven wealthiest industrial nations) to form the G8.

1999 Fighting resumes between Russian forces and rebels in Chechnya. Yeltsin resigns as president and appoints his prime minister, Vladimir Putin, as successor.

2002 Chechen terrorists take hostages in a Moscow theater.

2003 Referendum in Chechnya gives people in the province greater autonomy, but it remains part of Russia.

2004 (March) Putin is reelected as president of Russia.

2004 (May) The new president of Chechnya, Akhmad Kadyrov, is murdered in a bomb attack.

2004 (September) Chechen terrorists take hostages in a school in Beslan; the siege leaves 331 people dead.

2004 (November) Russia ratifies the Kyoto Protocol.

2006 Russia hosts the G8 summit in St. Petersburg.

Glossary

Allied forces the name given to the combined forces of Britain, France, the United States, and the Soviet Union during the World War II; they opposed Germany, Italy, and Japan

Bolshevik Party a Communist revolutionary group led by Vladimir Lenin, which seized power in the 1917 revolution in Russia

Chechen conflict a continuing war in the eastern part of the northern Caucasus in the south of Russia

Communism/Communist a social and political theory and system based on the ideas of Karl Marx in which the government owns property and industry, instead of private owners, and runs most parts of society; a Communist is a follower of communism

constitution a document that sets out the rights and duties of a government and its people

coup the overthrow of government by a group of people, usually using military force

czar the Russian emperor and head of the Russian royal family

deputy an elected representative in the parliament who debates and votes on whether or not to pass laws

ecology the study of the relationship of plants and animals to their environment

economy a community's system of using its resources to produce wealth

emigration the act of leaving one's own country to go to live permanently in another country

enclave a portion of territory surrounded by a larger territory; the people living in an enclave are often culturally and ethnically distinct from those in the larger territory

glasnost the policy of openness introduced by Mikhail Gorbachev in the Soviet Union in the mid-1980s

greenhouse gases gases in Earth's atmosphere that are believed to trap heat from the Sun and increase global warming

illiterate unable to read or write

immigration the act of arriving to live permanently in a country that is not one's country of origin

inflation a fall in the value of money in terms of the amount of goods it can buy

Kyoto Protocol an agreement made in 1997 in Kyoto, Japan, that requires participating countries to reduce their emissions of greenhouse gases by 2012 to an average of 5 percent below levels in 1990

lichens plants that grow as crusty patches or bushy growths on tree trunks and bare ground

literacy the ability to read and write

market economy a system in which individuals, rather than governments, make decisions about what to make and sell, based on and responding to what people want to buy.

NATO North Atlantic Treaty Organization; an international organization made up of the United States, Canada, and most European countries to guard international security

perestroika a plan introduced by Mikhail Gorbachev in the mid-1980s for restructuring the Soviet state

republic a state in which power does not belong to a royal family but rather to an elected government

serfs Russian peasants who were considered to belong to the person who owned the area in which they happened to be born

Soviet Union the country founded after the Russian Revolution, run by the Communist Party, made up of 15 republics (with a total population of 240 million), and covering one-sixth of the world's land

steppes vast, grassy plains

World Heritage site an area selected by a United Nations committee with the belief that it has value for the whole world and should be preserved

Further Information

BOOKS TO READ

Dando, William A. *Russia* (Modern World Nations). Chelsea House, 2007.

Hatt, Christine. *Catherine the Great* (Judge for Yourself). World Almanac Library, 2004.

Kort, Michael. *Russia* (Nations in Transition). Facts on File, 2004.

Lange, Brenda, and Charles J. Shields. *Vladimir Putin* (Major World Leaders). Chelsea House, 2007.

Libal, Autumn. *Women in the World of Russia* (Women's Issues, Global Trends). Mason Crest, 2005.

McNeese, Tim. *The Volga River* (Rivers in World History). Chelsea House, 2005.

Torchinsky, Oleg, and Angela Black. *Russia* (Cultures of the World). Benchmark Books, 2005.

Trumbauer, Lisa. *Russian Immigrants* (Immigration to the United States). Facts on File, 2004.

Uschan, Michael V. *The Beslan School Siege and Separatist Terrorism* (Terrorism in Today's World). World Almanac Library, 2005.

USEFUL WEB SITES

CIA World Factbook: Russia
www.cia.gov/cia/publications/factbook/geos/rs.html#Geo

Living Lakes: Lake Baikal
www.livinglakes.org/baikal/

Moscow, the Capital of Russia
www.ibiblio.org/sergei/Exs/Moscow/moscow.html

Nicholas and Alexandra
www.nicholasandalexandra.com/

PBS: The Face of Russia
www.pbs.org/weta/faceofrussia/

The State Hermitage Museum
www.hermitagemuseum.org/html_En/index.html

Publisher's note to educators and parents: Our editors have carefully reviewed these Web sites to ensure that they are suitable for children. Many Web sites change frequently, however, and we cannot guarantee that a site's future contents will continue to meet our high standards of quality and educational value. Be advised that children should be closely supervised whenever they access the Internet.

Index

Page numbers in **bold** indicate pictures.

About the Authors

Rob Bowden is a freelance educational writer and photographer with a university background in teaching geography and development studies. He has written and advised on many educational books and specializes in global environmental and social issues.

Born in Kirov in the former USSR, Galya Ransome is an experienced teacher of Russian with broad experience in interpreting and translating. She maintains a strong interest in developments in the post-Soviet era and visits Russia regularly. She has written and advised on many Russian books.